GROWING YOUR OWN CAPITAL

CONTROL HOW YOU FINANCE THE OPERATION, CREATE THE ULTIMATE LINE OF CREDIT, AND KEEP THE FARM IN THE FAMILY

GROWING YOUR OWN CAPITAL

CONTROL HOW YOU FINANCE THE OPERATION, CREATE THE ULTIMATE LINE OF CREDIT, AND KEEP THE FARM IN THE FAMILY

DAN ALLEN
RICHARD CANFIELD
JAYSON LOWE

ethos
collective

Published by Igniting Souls
PO Box 43, Powell, OH 43065
IgnitingSouls.com

LCCN: 2025902340
Paperback ISBN: 978-1-63680-462-0
Hardback ISBN: 978-1-63680-463-7
eBook ISBN: 978-1-63680-464-4

Available in paperback, hardcover, e-book, and audiobook.

All Scripture quotations, unless otherwise indicated, are taken from the Holy Bible, New International Version®, NIV®. Copyright © 1973, 1978, 1984 by Biblica, Inc.™ Used by permission of Zondervan. All rights reserved worldwide.

Any Internet addresses (websites, blogs, etc.) and telephone numbers printed in this book are offered as a resource. They are not intended in any way to be or imply an endorsement by Igniting Souls, nor does Igniting Souls vouch for the content of these sites and numbers for the life of this book.

Some names and identifying details may have been changed to protect the privacy of individuals.

The superscript symbol IP listed throughout this book is known as the unique certification mark created and owned by Instant IP™. Its use signifies that the corresponding expression (words, phrases, chart, graph, etc.) has been protected by Instant IP™ via smart contract. Instant IP™ is designed with the patented smart contract solution (US Patent: 11,928,748), which creates an immutable time-stamped first layer and fast layer identifying the moment in time an idea is filed on the blockchain. This solution can be used in defending intellectual property protection. Infringing upon the respective intellectual property, i.e., IP, is subject to and punishable in a court of law.

Table of Contents

Part Three: Harvest

Foreword

Farming is more than a profession—it's a way of life built on hard work, risk, and perseverance. Few understand the financial challenges farmers face like Dan. Having spent years in the agricultural world, he has seen firsthand the struggles farmers endure: unpredictable markets, rising costs, and the constant pressure to finance equipment, land, and operations. His appreciation for the commitment and resilience it takes to succeed in this industry forms the foundation of this book.

At the same time, Dan brings a deep understanding of the Infinite Banking Concept™ (IBC) and its powerful potential to transform the way farmers manage their money. His dedication to learning, applying, and teaching IBC shines through as he offers practical ways farmers can create more financial control, stability, and legacy. His knowledge in this space is both well-earned and deeply rooted, and he has a passion for helping farmers take back the reins of their financial future.

This book is an invitation to think differently, to explore new money tools, and to challenge the traditional models that often leave farmers struggling. Dan has taken a meaningful step in connecting two worlds—farming and infinite banking—and anyone reading this will walk away with a fresh perspective on what's possible.

Mary Jo Irmen
Author of *Farming Without the Bank*
& *Life Without the Bank*
Authorized IBC Practitioner

Introduction

by R. Nelson Nash

Transcribed from "This Is Nelson Nash: The Creator of The Infinite Banking Concept" and "How to Make Financial Moves That Will Make Others Jealous!" Recorded in January 2017

We behave on the basis on which we are taught, and we are taught absolute nonsense.

Back when I was three or four years old, my dad was a tenant farmer in Madison County, Georgia. It took a lot of labor to do the work at the time, but look at what a single person can do today! The difference is capital.

Here's the thing: My oldest daughter works for the Auburn University extension service. They are out there teaching farmers how to grow crops with scientific precision, but every farmer today is highly capitalized. Nowhere do they teach people how to grow their own capital.

Let's contrast that with teaching people how to grow cattle. Cattle consume feed, cow chow. If I were a farmer growing cattle and I bought my cow chow off the market, you guys would laugh me out of the county! You need to be growing your own cow chow.

Well, in the same way, you need to be growing your own capital. But that's not thought of.

I spent twenty-eight years in the National Guard. There were only a couple of weeks every year when we were on active duty at camp.

Guess what was happening with the camp's equipment during the off-season? It was sitting there for fifty weeks! You need to keep these things busy, or the equipment starts to fail.

All your money is doing the same thing. It sits there until you decide to use it again. Couple that with the fact that in the farming community today, a lot of your money is borrowed.

During my forestry days, I was pioneering the technique of clearing the land with Caterpillar tractors for tree-growing purposes, and the payments on those three tractors were attention-getting, to say the least. It took other equipment to get the tractors into position to do their job. A Caterpillar tractor sitting still is the most worthless piece of equipment I can imagine. It's just collecting rust and dust.

It's just like the condition of farmers.

People in the eighties discovered that they could put money into a policy, and after several years, they could surrender it without tax consequences. The IRS said it was foul play to disguise something when it wasn't designed to do that, so they came up with the idea of a modified endowment contract.

One of the side effects is that people keep thinking life insurance is a product of the IRS code, but it is not. In the US, the IRS code has only been around since 1913. Life insurance is older than the United States!

We have to address the disease that infects the minds of most people regarding life insurance. You think you don't want to pay life insurance premiums because that is a bad place to put money, but life insurance is separate from the IRS. This is the hardest way of thinking to overcome because it has been instilled in the minds of most adults. People want to pay as little as they can and get the most coverage as they can.

In essence, the Infinite Banking Concept is ridiculously simple, but it becomes complicated by the mindset the general public has. They think that this can't be true because it's so simple. You've got to learn to secede from the way the world believes. When you do, you create a microcosm that's all yours. The more you see, the more you realize you didn't truly see before.

We've got to have a starting point. We're going to use the tool of life insurance to carry out the concept of banking. We need to understand how that works. The more you capitalize, the better. However, you've got to build a system to accommodate everything that you do. There's no way that one policy will do that; it's impossible.

It took me thirteen years to get rid of the banks, but so what? Those thirteen years would have gone by anyway. Once you get rid of them, it's such a different life.

But be careful. When you've "arrived," you've quit thinking (as in arriving in knowledge). Learning should be a continuous process in your life. Otherwise, it's not much of a life. When people have the arrival syndrome, it turns off their ability to receive inspiration. In reality, you've never truly arrived. This is a process that keeps going.

The banking function should be controlled at the individual level. It's the best way to pass the medium of exchange onto the next generation.

PART ONE

Seed

1

Planting the Foundation: An Introduction to IBC

The life of a farmer isn't easy.

You worry about market fluctuations, unpredictable weather, taxes, old equipment, and the challenges of working with livestock. That's not the end; your list of troubles continues.

The life of a farmer also isn't cheap.

Fuel, equipment, seed, livestock, medicine, vet services, and fencing materials, not to mention the land itself. Every little (or big) expense adds up until you feel like you'll never be able to make a profit.

You have so much capital tied up for such a small return. Even when it's not the right time from the market perspective, you have to pay operating loans. You may even find it challenging to work with multiple family members.

As you wait for the market to correct itself, your capital is all locked up in your business (such as in land, machines, seeds, livestock, or fertilizer), leaving you without immediate access to funds. Although it's your money, you can't use it to pay off loans or buy new equipment. You've invested time and resources into your farm, yet you're left waiting.

Meanwhile, you're trying to keep up with the latest improvements in agriculture while hoping you don't break the bank. You don't want to be left behind, but you also don't know if the investment is worth it for your financial future.

Every day, you hope your biggest fears won't be realized: crop failures, land prices increasing and large corporations buying property in a flash, having to depend on government programs, the loss of a family member heavily involved in the operation, needing to sell or go bankrupt, or placing the family's legacy on the chopping block.

You're not alone.

Reports across North America confirm what you already feel: The rising cost of operating, the interest spikes, the input inflation—they're eating farms alive. Bankruptcies are up. The pressure is high. And the banks? They keep getting richer.

As reported by the American Farm Bureau Federation, interest rate expenses for farmers have spiked significantly in the last several years, increasing by about 43 percent between 2022 and 2023.

These issues are not just isolated to the United States.

The Canadian Federation of Farming's 2023-2024 Farm Financial Health Report reveals that despite the farming sector contributing billions of dollars to Canada's GDP in 2022, total operating expenses increased by 19.9 percent in the same year.

We get it. With all these numbers, the future can feel daunting, to say the least.

You simply want to provide a good life for your family, then pass the farm on to future generations without giving them the hardships you've had to face. With your current financial pressures, you wonder if that's even possible.

The idea of keeping the farm with the family remains a dream for many folks like you. Farming is a profession of trial and error. You're always refining, always adapting, because this isn't just a business; it's your passion, a way of life you truly love.

Here's the good news. There's a different way to keep that dream alive. Not a quick fix but a powerful process. One that hundreds of farmers like you are already using. It's called the Infinite Banking Concept™ (IBC).

Just like bad government policies, your finances can make or break your farm's success, and not all of those factors are under your control. You can do everything right, but if the weather isn't favorable or prices rise, you risk losing profit— or worse, losing your farm.

It's overwhelming.

You've spent a lifetime trying to build a successful farm, and you deserve to have that dream come true. It's time to challenge how you finance your business.

What Is IBC?

IBC is more than just a way to grow capital. Similar to farming, it's a lifestyle. It is a way to finance every purchase you will make for the rest of your life and your family's lives for generations to come.

The process is ridiculously simple.

First, you customize and apply for a dividend-paying whole life insurance policy (or a system of policies) with a reputable (ideally a mutual) life insurance company. Then, you fund the policy with premium payments. This can be accomplished with some basic one-on-one coaching to redirect your existing cash flows, profits, and even existing savings. The results of this activity will immediately begin to build up an asset called cash value, capital you can access and control.

You are not just buying life insurance; you are building a financial system. This cash value is very similar to the equity you have stored in your land holdings. Once you have strategically implemented this, instant cash value is created.

From this place of total control, you can borrow from your system, using the cash value as collateral. These aren't like bank loans. There are no repayment schedules and no banker breathing down your neck. You decide when and how to pay them back, not the bank, and not the insurance company.

These are unstructured loans. This gives you complete autonomy over your farm finances and, for many farm families, revolutionizes how they keep both their money and the farm for generations.

You repay these policy loans on your terms, not some commercial banker's rules. You pay back the interest to the life insurance company you co-own instead of to a third-party lender. Every dollar that you repay instantly becomes accessible for your next major purchase.

Meanwhile, the entire time you are using the life insurance company's money to fire your third-party lenders, your cash value grows consistently like clockwork, without market risk or interruption. No matter how much you borrow against it, the life insurance company you co-own (your business partner) grows the cash value.

Dividends are paid to you every single year the company is profitable, regardless of whether or not you have an outstanding policy loan.

Unlike a bad year of weather that could cripple your farm profits, these contracts are unaffected. You pay interest to the company as the loan is considered an invested asset to them. You and the other participating whole life owners are the only ones who benefit from all of their assets, making the policy loan you take out an asset to them.

This is one of the areas where they strategically and securely put money to work consistently. Unlike the loans your farm operation is used to dealing with, this is an "unstructured" loan, meaning you have total control over when and how much you repay. The life company cannot force you to send payments. You must rely on yourself to manage that responsibility in the same way you rely on yourself to manage your farm operation.

This is one of the key reasons this method of farm financing is perfect for hard-working farmers just like you.

Once you fully utilize your policy by developing solid habits through practice, you can open up additional policies to continue storing the flow of financial energy that passes through your operation. Within just a few years, the positive impact can be drastic! This builds your financial flexibility and expands your system. Imagine the wealth increase a family of four would have if each person had two policies instead of one.

Your opportunities are limitless!

IBC is a process that changes how you think. By using whole life insurance, you can borrow against these constantly accumulating assets as needed. With each step, you gain control of capital and your legacy by eliminating traditional banks.

With a bank, you would have to start over every time you take out a new loan. As you pay back your loan, your interest benefits only the bank and its stockholders. Once the loan is paid, you have to repeat the process. Each time, you jump through the various hoops and challenges to convince them to grant you approval for the loan.

We've been there. It's a frustrating process of tracking down documents and answering Mickey Mouse questions when you should be operating a tractor and focusing on your operation.

Think about it:

Whose money is the banker lending?

a. Their own money

b. Your money

The answer is b. The bank is lending out the money you and others deposit, not any capital that belongs to them.

Say you deposit $50,000. The banker doesn't let that cash sit still. They put it to work and lend it to someone else to buy a tractor. When that person makes a purchase, the receiver puts it right back into the bank. Then, the bank lends it out again. Using their technology, they can put your money to work in seconds to create new streams of payments with more incoming interest.

In the same way, a farmer plants seeds and can harvest something that is thousands of times greater than the seed; recognize this is what the commercial banks are doing with the deposits of everyone you know. The banker makes money from every payment that hits their books. They profit off of your hard-earned money, and they will continue to do so for each of your family members and your farm unless you change it.

Our mentor, Nelson Nash, was clear:

"Someone or some institution must perform the function of banking in your life; it can and should be you."

Every liability you have is an asset on someone else's balance sheet.

We've been taught that loans and debt are bad for consumers. That is because most people are always the ones borrowing. However, if you own the loan and the stream of payments, the loans become an asset, just as they show up on the balance sheet of your local bank.

With your banking system, you can essentially "recapture" the interest for your benefit. When you want to take out a policy loan, you pay it back with the same or greater interest rate that a third-party lender would have charged you.

The difference now is that you pay interest back to an entity you have a co-owner relationship with, the life insurance company. Guess what? It is co-owned by other people just like you. The types of families that care about protecting the ones they love, and you all get to share in these benefits.

Now, if you are a good steward and put in some extra interest, it can go towards expanding your system. Just like you would send extra payments to pay off a bank loan, this additional interest can become extra premiums in your system of policies. The result of your new method of banking is that it builds additional capital that you own and control.

The more you repeat this habit, the more policies you will have. The more wealth you increase, the more stable and robust your banking business will become. This process is similar to acquiring more chunks of land in order to scale the farm operation and expand the profit potential.

Each of these assets (participating dividend-paying policies) is surrounded by tax-free death benefits. This creates perpetual motion with your family members and can ensure the farm stays where it belongs because you put that death benefit right back into your policies. Keep in mind, this wealth will only build if we teach the right habits to the next generation.

Think of IBC this way: Paying interest to someone else is like walking into a headwind. You can get to your destination, but it requires more effort to fight against it. That headwind happens when you borrow from banks.

If you're going to be paying the interest anyway, you might as well pay it back to a company you co-own so you can get rid of the headwind pushing against you. Over time, the result is a tailwind, and with the wind at your back, you can truly soar!

No matter what happens with market fluctuations, your policy and your pool of capital continually improve year by year. You become the banker of a system that only you control, cutting out the middleman who only wants to make money off you. Your family and farm operation automatically become more self-sufficient and vastly more protected. Keeping the farm in the family becomes drastically easier with the implementation of this strategy.

Even better, your loans are accessible at any time. You don't have to wait for credit checks or lengthy application processes. As long as your money is in that policy, it grows tax-free.

Why IBC Works for Farmers

Consider how a crop insurance program protects against losses. When bad weather harms your crops, the program provides a financial safety net, ensuring you can get back on your feet without losing everything. It's Risk Management 101 for your farming operation.

In the same way, IBC builds a pool of capital you can use if an emergency threatens your farm or your family. As the cash value builds, often much faster than you realize, you have access to more and more capital. An unexpected medical emergency or equipment failure does not become a burden as you borrow the money from a system you own and control.

If a family member dies, their death benefit provides a much-needed influx of cash when you need it the most. This safety net, just like the crop insurance program, can be the difference between keeping the farm in the family or having to sell it all at an auction. Instead of struggling with what to do next, you are prepared to face the future.

The Infinite Banking Concept empowers you with unparalleled financial benefits, including:

- Control over your finances
- Peace of mind for your family farm
- A volatility buffer from market, political, and even weather risks
- Recaptured interest
- Guaranteed growth
- Tax-free death benefits
- Flexible loan terms, unlike anything you have ever experienced before
- A rock-solid foundation of financial habits
- Generational wealth

To further illustrate, consider the protection of having a variety of livestock. If disease or market fluctuations affect one species, your diversity ensures a steady source of income. Likewise, multiple insurance policies on family members provide the same kind of diversity.

The more people insured in your system, the more capital you have to borrow from and the more diversified your risk.

If one of you takes a financial hit, you are all there to support each other. If one family member passes, the death benefit can go back into the system. This allows you to maintain stability in your family's needs and operations, a constant requirement for additional capital. The result is that you get to keep building your wealth while ensuring a legacy for each of your loved ones.

Consider how much money you and your family have made in the past year. What percent of it do you still have access to? And what percent do you have of all the money you made throughout your life?

Who did all the work to earn that income?

That's why you need IBC. Starting here, you can take control of your financial system and recapture the interest you've been losing up until now. You'll never get your money back, but you can gain control of what financial energy flows through your hands from this moment on.

The reality is this: you work hard every day only to see your money continually line the pockets of someone else.

Although your financial security should be well-earned, factors out of your control steal profits and leave you with stress and worry. IBC, when the correct habits are implemented properly, will help you grow your capital so you can pass your farm down to future generations.

In the end, your business is the backbone of our lives. As the food you produce feeds the world, the world becomes a place where others can live and be fruitful. Without you, we quite simply would not be able to exist. It's time you had the financial security you deserve in return, one that you can get by implementing the IBC process. More capital, more control, more security, more legacy.

You deserve a financial system that can support you just like you support everyone else.

2

A Farmer's Journey: Dan's Story

Growing up on the family farm, I learned all about hard work.

In my opinion, there's no better place to grow up. It was a great place to live and learn. Instead of being given the choice of whether we wanted to work or not, we were expected to, and I feel blessed to have discovered the values of discipline and dedication early in life.

One of my favorite memories is working and playing with the animals. We didn't have quads or UTVs back then, but we had horses, and I can remember spending hours riding for both pleasure and farming.

Horses became a big part of my life. I raised and trained them, and I had the privilege of teaching horsemanship classes to children. I loved learning each animal's unique personality, and there was no greater joy than witnessing how a person could become more comfortable around a horse and master skills that once felt out of reach.

At age forty-six, I took a horsemanship training course, and during those few weeks, I realized I knew nothing about horses. Sure, I had used them, but I really didn't understand them. What the instructor could do with my horse in minutes would have taken me several months to learn. Even though I was around them my whole life, I still didn't know how horses worked.

My family had the same relationship with money. We used money all the time, but we didn't truly understand how it worked. As a result, we struggled financially, and I remember thinking, "There has to be a better way."

As I went through grade school, I aspired to be a farmer, so after graduating high school, I studied Vocational Agriculture for two years at Lakeland College.

At the age of twenty, I started farming. I was determined to make a difference, and I worked hard building a hog barn and a house in the first year. Then, I started to raise piglets. I was doing all that with borrowed money. In the first year or so, farmers don't make enough to pay those loans back.

The financing company told me not to worry; the payment I owed would be added to the end of my loan. I would only have to pay the interest charges. Some of those loans had a twenty-nine-year amortization period, so when you think about the compounding interest, it was no small amount.

Two years into my journey as a farmer, prime interest rates went up to 21.5 percent, so I was paying over 23 percent on my operating loans for my farm business. Later on in life, I would find out that I wasn't the only one drastically impacted by these rates. The late R. Nelson Nash, who created the Infinite Banking Concept himself, was almost destroyed by this rate hike. One of the things I remember during the height of the interest rates was one fall, one-third of the cash crop production on the family farm went to pay just the annual payment on the combine we used to take that crop off.

Just think about the other costs of raising and harvesting those crops that had to come from only the remaining two-thirds of the cash crops. It's clear how difficult it was to make a go of farming at the time, and you might even see parallels in your own story.

As a result of these issues, the income from my farming operation wasn't enough to cover the costs I was incurring, so I had to start working off the farm to make ends meet. That was the only way I was able to get by, and it meant working two full-time jobs. That lifestyle got old very quickly, and I was basically working one job to pay for the losses on the farm.

Again, I was thinking, "There has to be a better way."

Gradually, I phased myself out of raising piglets and focused more on the other job. I kept living on the farm and helping my family as much as I could with our cow-calf operations and cash crops.

As I reflect on those times, here are some thoughts I had:

- I had gone to college and studied farming, which included financing and building a business plan. Even with that, working hard wasn't enough to ensure success. None of this education taught me how I could control the financing . . . it only taught me how to present my farm's information to my local bank to get access to their money.

- Money had a cost, and because of how I financed my business, I could not control that cost.

- Planning was necessary, but all elements needed to be addressed in that plan.

- When I started my business, I didn't have enough information. I should have spent more time with successful pig farmers, asking questions and learning from their experiences.

- Even though I had studied how to operate a business like this, no one told me how money worked, and I didn't think to ask or find out. I didn't realize how important it is to a business.

A few years after I started my second job, it became apparent I would need to step completely out of the family farm to focus fully on my other career. Other than helping around the farm on my time off, I was no longer a farmer. For several decades, the second career went on to be very successful.

Based on my experience on the farm, I was determined to get out of debt and pay cash for the things I needed. So, I worked hard, and by the grace of God, I reached that position before I turned fifty.

I had arrived at the place in life where I thought this was as good as it gets from a financial perspective!

What I noticed was that even though I was paying cash for the things I needed or wanted in life, I wasn't keeping much of the money I earned. Therefore, I started to search for what I could do differently. By this time, I realized I needed to own assets that would increase in value and provide income for me and my family.

To accomplish this, I bought two pieces of real estate: a condo in a resort and a quarter section of agricultural land. The intent with the first was to earn income from rentals, and the intent with the land was to produce hay to sell.

How do you think I paid for both assets?

That's right; I paid cash. Then, I sat back and waited for the money to come in. With the condo, it took about five years to be cash flow positive, and once it finally got there, we had a worldwide pandemic.

Great.

With the land, some years were good, and some years not so much. It depended on the amount of rain, the condition the hay was put up in, whether the hay was rained on while drying, and the price I got for the hay.

As a result, cash flow was variable with both assets, and many reasons were out of my control. All along, I kept wondering if there was a better way! It seemed like if I invested in the right opportunity where all these uncontrollable factors aligned in my favor, the assets I purchased might ultimately work out to my advantage.

However, there were a lot of "ifs" involved.

These weren't the only things I did. I also bought precious metals and stones, among many other attempts to build capital. No matter how much I experimented, nothing gave me a sense of peace about creating a source of income I could depend on later in life.

Then, one Saturday morning, I was driving west along the Yellowhead Highway in Alberta, Canada. The radio was tuned to my favorite talk show when a strange infomercial came on.

"Be your own banker!" the announcer said.

"Yeah, right," I thought. "How's that gonna work?"

But, instead of changing the channel, I listened.

He continued, "Come to our event and learn more about Becoming Your Own Banker."

I was skeptical but intrigued. I had to work the day of the event, so I called my wife, Barb, and asked her to go. The next week, as I waited for her to come home, I wondered what she thought of this process—and if it was as life-changing as it sounded.

Finally, she walked in the door. "Dan," she said, "I think this will work!"

So, in 2013, we began the process of Becoming Your Own Banker. My wife and I were both approved for our first dividend-paying whole life insurance policies at the beginning of 2014. Over the next few years, we also started policies on our children. As the value of our money grew, I often thought, "I wish I had heard about this twenty years ago!"

I had finally found the "better way" I had been searching for!

Inspired by this process and how it was helping my family, I attended an event hosted by the founder, R. Nelson Nash. Over time, I saw people's faces light up as they discovered what my wife and I had learned: this works!

It was then that I realized, "I want to teach others how to do this. THIS is my calling."

So, in 2017, I became an Authorized Infinite Banking Practitioner with the Nelson Nash Institute, and it was one of the best decisions of my life. I had the honor of meeting Nelson Nash for the first time in 2014, and I will never forget the last time I saw him. It was February 2019, about six weeks before he passed. He truly changed my life.

I work with many talented and inspiring people, including Jayson Lowe, the man on the radio I heard while driving down the highway. Jayson Lowe and Richard Canfield taught the educational event my wife went to at the start, and Jayson became my coach in this process.

Today, my clients are business owners, farmers, and employees ranging from eighteen to seventy-four. The one thing they all have in common is a growth mindset.

They're always looking for a better way to do something. They're not comfortable with the status quo, and they often ask me, "When it comes to money, how can I be better tomorrow than I am today?"

Teaching them how to become their own banker is the answer to that question. Becoming your own banker allows you to reach a place of financial peace, a place with enough money to sustain you later in life, AND one that makes sure your family is looked after for generations to come.

This is why I do what I do.

Becoming Your Own Banker changed my life, and I know it will change yours, too.

PART TWO

Grow

3

Fertilizing Financial Stability

I n your farming life, you will face unexpected challenges. That's a guarantee.

Unpredictable weather can delay planting or harvesting. Excessive rain may cause crops to rot or drown, while droughts threaten their growth.

The exact shift in the market or public opinion can't be foreseen, so you will have to face what comes, whether you're ready or not. Despite this, there are ways to prepare for crises, and you shouldn't be surprised when we say IBC is one of the best ones.

IBC provides what you might call Financial Fertilizer[IP]. Just as fertilizer supplies plants with nutrients to make them stronger, IBC sets your financial foundation, "soil," with the perfect conditions for accelerated growth to make you more resilient against unforeseen challenges.

Without fertilizer, a plant grows slower, has nutrient deficiencies, and develops a weaker structure. The plant will still grow, but it may not be as healthy as a plant with fertilizer. Ultimately, you may sacrifice a large part of your yield come harvest time.

In much the same way, IBC gives a boost to your financial system, building it stronger and faster than before. Without it, you can still build capital, but it will take more time and effort.

The thing is, we can't always know the best way to do something. We may spend years with our tried-and-true technique or our favorite equipment, but until we experiment with something new, we will stay in our old ways.

Take Dan's story of working with horses for years and then taking a horsemanship class. It took an outside perspective to realize there was a better way.

As Daniel J. Boorstin said, "The greatest obstacle to discovering the shape of the earth, the continents, and the oceans was not ignorance but the illusion of knowledge."

We think we know the best way, but we soon realize that what we thought was Financial Fertilizer was actually draining our resources without providing true growth.

One worry we hear clients express is whether they are insurable. Maybe because of health issues, age, or other uncontrollable factors, they wonder if they could even start this process if they can't be insured.

To that, we say the best thing to do is try. People are often accepted even when they didn't expect to be.

If you're not insurable, however, that does not mean you can't start this process. You can open a policy on someone else, like your spouse or kids. This way, you keep building policies and growing your cash value.

If you're single and have no kids, you can still open policies on other people.

Think about any person in whom you have a financial interest, for example, your business partners, key farmhands, or parents who work alongside you. We can agree that you have a financial incentive for wanting them to be alive.

Without this financial interest, the life insurance company will not approve you to have a policy on this person. This is why people go in on real estate together; as far as the company sees it, you have an economic motivation for this friend to be alive.

We get this question often: Who should we start with?

We always say the matriarch or the patriarch of the immediate family. The adults are the main financial providers for the family, and because they have more income, they can qualify for larger policies.

Take Dan's family: he, as the patriarch, started the policy because he could put money into the policy better than his kids could.

In the dismal event that the matriarch or patriarch passes, the death benefit provides relief that goes back into the system. As the oldest member, statistically, he or she will "graduate" before everyone else, and his or her insurance will create a cascade effect that will ripple through the family system.

Once the matriarch and patriarch are covered, you can start covering the kids and then the grandchildren. If they are young, you will be the one funding the system. When they are adults, you can decide whether you maintain control of the policy and establish clear rules for ongoing participation or if you sign it over to them. Either way, they can open more policies on themselves as they age and their income rises.

Imagine an account where every time you "deposited" $1, you had $2 or even $3 at the end of the year. How much opportunity would that create for you? While it won't happen overnight, this process, when done properly, creates exactly this type of environment.

Nelson Nash often told the story of a policy he started in 1959 at twenty-eight years old. When Nelson passed away in 2019, this policy had 59.5 years under its belt. In 2006–2009, Nelson wanted to prove a point. He asked the life insurance company to send him his annual dividend profits as a check rather than buying more whole life insurance (the most effective usage of the dividend for compounding potential). Each check was more than ten times the annual premium.

In those four years, Nelson recovered 100 percent of the lifetime worth of premiums he had funded, and the policy was still growing despite the global financial crisis. Nelson often said it was a "peaceful, stress-free way of life when you get rid of the banks."

How to Think Like a Farmer (Who Is Also a Banker)

Consider a system that your family has complete control over. In a few short years, every dollar of premium you fund creates a bigger amount of equity in the form of cash value in your system. Each year that goes by, it is engineered to become more efficient.

If you had a piece of equipment essential to your farming operation, I imagine you would take good care of it, maintain it regularly, and make everyone in the operation (such as family members and farm hands) very aware of how important that piece of equipment is to your success and even survival as an operation.

In the same way, you will make sure everyone learns and recognizes the critical importance of the system of strategic capital you are building for the multiple lives insured.

People often worry about having to pay the premium, but the truth is, the premium is the *solution*, not the problem.

You will want to pay the premium; in fact, you will seek out ways to fund as much as you can because the more you do so, the more capital you can access.

If you are growing crops, then you need seed. No seeds, no yield potential, no harvest. You have to acquire the seeds and plant them to get the result you want. Funding premiums is very similar to replacing your seeds each spring, so you can create something of real value.

Think of how excited you get on payday. With more access to capital, you might be imagining that house you're saving for or that piece of land you could buy.

You should have that same level of excitement with IBC. When you pay premiums, you are paying yourself and your loved ones in the future. You can look forward to paying it because you are allowing your future self to have more capital and greater efficiency to make business decisions. This mindset switch is the key factor to start thinking like a farmer who owns a bank.

To be clear, patience is required. You are not going to build your system overnight. You likely won't be able to put a down payment on a new tractor the same year you start your policy, depending on your circumstances and your level of commitment. But it's not about the now; it's about the future. You are building the financial future that serves you and future generations.

All it costs is time.

A Lifeline for the Unexpected: Dan's Story

Unexpected illnesses are no fun.

A few years ago, my wife traveled to eastern Canada to look after my daughter's house and pets, including a dog she took on frequent walks. Afterward, my wife flew to a five-day family gathering on Vancouver Island (West Coast) before returning home.

Within a few days, she was suddenly exhausted all the time. At first, we thought nothing of it. After all, she just had a busy couple of weeks with lots of traveling, so it made sense that she was tired.

But then, one night while we were getting ready for bed, she told me there was something wonky with her heart. I checked her pulse and felt that her heart rhythm was all over the map. We went to the hospital, and the hospital staff was eventually able to get her rhythm back to normal.

My wife went home that night, but a few days later, something wasn't right. This time, she was showing symptoms of a heart attack.

For background information, my wife comes from a healthy family. Her mother lived to be over one hundred, so I always knew she was going to outlive me. After years of this kind of thinking, these health issues were completely unexpected and very scary.

We went to the hospital again, and while in the waiting room, I happened to spot a bruise on her ankle. Since then, I have learned that it is a typical tick bite bullseye. We were incredibly lucky she had this symptom because it was easier to pinpoint what the issue was: Lyme disease.

We live in the prairies. Our area doctors, unfortunately, don't have much experience with Lyme disease. With my wife's many travels, it was unclear how or where she got the bite, but it definitely wasn't here. She was showing other symptoms, like a rash on her body.

While the doctor admitted she did not have much knowledge or experience in treating Lyme disease, she immediately began researching the topic, then prescribed antibiotics. We were all doing our own research to figure out what we could do. We contacted doctors familiar with the disease and talked with other people who'd previously had Lyme disease, while doctors sent her bloodwork to Germany.

A few days after my wife finished her four-week antibiotic treatment, she relapsed. Once again, we worried about her heart symptoms. This happened several times throughout her recovery, and it took a lot of care to get her back to a stable place.

Not everyone is as lucky as we were to catch the disease so early. The longer it takes to recognize the illness, the worse it can be for people. We consider ourselves very blessed!

Okay, now, what does this have to do with IBC?

Here's the thing: While going through this experience, one thing that became apparent was the sheer cost. Between out-of-pocket medical costs and missing work time, treatment and healthcare cost money even with insurance.

Fortunately, IBC provided a safety net.

This situation was unexpected. In a matter of days, our lives were turned completely upside down, and there was no way we could have prepared for it.

No way other than IBC.

The policy I already had in place was increasing in cash value every day. At the time of my wife's Lyme disease, it was $108 a day. Even if I incurred more costs, I had access to capital to pay them off. I knew that when I accessed that capital, the money continued to grow uninterrupted.

My banking system was preparing my family for any future emergencies.

Unforeseen Market Pressures

In the 2010s, A&W Canada made a move that sent a ripple through the farming community by marketing "hormone-free" beef. Many farmers called out the company for implying that beef with hormones is worse for your health, which influenced public opinion away from farms that didn't use the more expensive hormone-free techniques.

Because there was not enough hormone-free beef in Canada, the company had to outsource to reach its standards, switching from fresh, local beef to frozen, imported beef.

As a result, many farmers felt more pressure to fit their businesses into the mold of what public opinion wanted, even if that was not financially attainable for them. They worried about the future of their farms if they chose not to switch over.

Unfortunately, these kinds of crises happen. Market changes are out of your control, yet you are the one to face the consequences. Without Financial Fertilizer, you could be left anxious, overwhelmed, and underappreciated.

Think about how this situation would be different if you had your own banking system. No one wants to face a lower demand for their product, but with readily accessible capital, you wouldn't have to worry when the market suddenly changes.

As the world around you feels unstable, IBC provides a sense of security you can't get anywhere else. IBC changes the way you think about your finances. After all, IBC is not a product you buy but a process you learn and implement as a lifestyle moving forward. You reconsider your responsibility in choosing how you finance, no longer going to banks for your capital.

Of course, we're not getting into the debate of whether hormone-free beef is healthier. There are many factors to consider, and traditional farming practices should not be rejected as the advertising campaign portrayed.

The most important lesson from this experience is how critical it is to be prepared for whatever comes.

Many factors impact the success of your farm, and it is impossible to predict all of them. The best way to be prepared is to be vigilant and build a safety net that can catch you if you stumble and fall. Your Financial Fertilizer lays a solid foundation for your financing practices.

Family illnesses, droughts, supply chain crises, and equipment failure are only some of the problems that having your own Infinite Banking system can support. The unexpected doesn't have to be scary, not when you have ready-access capital to ease the financial burden and get you back on your feet.

4

Two Farmers, Two Different Futures

In the same prairie town, not far from the same dusty crossroads, two men were born just twenty minutes apart. Same hospital, same calloused hands by the time they were ten. You'd be forgiven for thinking they were brothers.

In a way, they were brothers by land, by lineage, by the rhythm of planting and praying and harvesting. What happened next in their lives couldn't have been more different.

Both inherited six hundred acres of good, workable soil. Both faced the same spring floods, the same July hail, the same machinery repairs, and the same rising fuel costs. At the same point in time, early forties, with a few gray hairs sprouting like thistles, they each wanted to accumulate $500,000 to keep their farms running and growing.

One reached for the same old toolbox his father had used. The other built a new one.

Farmer #1: The Banker's Man

Meet Ray.

Ray did what farmers have always done when times call for capital: He scraped together what he could and tucked it away in the local bank, or he applied for loans. Fifty thousand dollars a year. He was disciplined. Old-school. Kept a ledger by hand. Each deposit felt like a victory, a sacrifice even, because let's be honest, what farmer has *extra* money just lying around?

It took him ten years. Ten years of good yields, tight belts, and no new combine. At the end, he had $500,000 saved. You could almost hear the cash sighing, sitting quietly in his savings account, earning a modest 4 percent after taxes . . . when the rates even cooperated.

Unfortunately, Ray couldn't afford to leave the money untouched. His need for capital was constant: equipment, supplies, fuel, feed, repairs. Some years, he withdrew from his savings. Other years, he borrowed from someone else's bank. In both cases, the result was the same: a permanent transfer of money away from him, his family, and his farm.

Each time Ray dipped into his savings, he lost compounding. Each time he borrowed, he got a monthly reminder from the bank—on their terms, not his. Every withdrawal or payment was a leak in the bucket. The more water he hauled in, the more leaked out the side.

Every dollar Ray put in the bank helped someone, no question. The question was: *who?* The bank earned interest. Its shareholders pocketed dividends. Ray got the interest he was promised, a few crumbs off the table he helped build.

This example shows the simplicity of putting $50,000 into a savings account for ten years (at the same time each year) and then no longer adding funds and letting it grow. In this example, the money grows uninterrupted each year (meaning no withdrawals happened during the year), and we are assuming 4 percent net after taxes on interest earnings.

Ray as the Banker's Man[IP] loses money to the bank because he is not in control of his financial system.

Year	Annual Deposit	Value at 4% Annual ROR
1	$50,000	$52,000
2	$50,000	$106,080
3	$50,000	$162,323
4	$50,000	$220,816
5	$50,000	$281,648
6	$50,000	$344,914
7	$50,000	$410,711
8	$50,000	$479,139
9	$50,000	$550,305
10	$50,000	$624,317
15	$0	$759,577
20	$0	$924,142
25	$0	$1,124,360

30	$0	$1,367,956
35	$0	$1,664,328

Farmer #2: The Banker He Became

Now, meet Jake.

Jake read something once, an idea from a Southern forester named R. Nelson Nash. The book was titled *Becoming Your Own Banker*. The idea was simple: "To control how you finance all the things you need throughout a lifetime and to recapture the interest you would have otherwise paid to someone else's bank."

The very first principle Jake learned was, "You finance everything you buy. Either you pay interest to someone else, or you give up the interest you could have earned."

Jake wanted to change how that worked on his farm.

So he took the same fifty grand Ray saved each year and put it somewhere else: a dividend-paying whole life insurance policy from a mutual company. Not because he needed insurance—he already had that—but because this kind of policy came with a living benefit: cash value he could access anytime, without begging a banker to say yes.

Here's what Jake did differently . . . and what changed everything:

From day one, Jake accessed policy loans from the life insurance company to finance what his farm needed. These weren't like bank loans. There were no repayment schedules. No banker breathing down his neck.

These were *unstructured* loans; Jake could repay on *his* time, not someone else's. A blessing, especially in a business where hail can erase your profits in ten minutes or a drought can starve your crop all summer.

While he borrowed, something incredible happened: Jake's total cash value kept rising. Every day, uninterrupted, the loan didn't touch it. The liens were on the death benefit of the policy, not his farming equipment. The asset kept growing. He could repay the loans whenever the farm allowed. When he did, he instantly regained access to the repaid amount *plus more*. No penalties, no taxes, no locked doors.

By year ten, Jake had paid $500,000, just like Ray. But Jake had access to over $500,000, *and* his capital never stopped compounding. That's because he used the life insurance company's money, not his. His policy kept growing while his farm kept running.

What if the unthinkable happened? A tractor rollover, a highway accident, a fatality—Jake's family wouldn't be left scrambling. They'd be met with a large, tax-free death benefit. It would arrive when it was needed most.

A cushion in the chaos. A legacy, not a liability.

Jake didn't wait ten or fifteen years to start benefiting. He used it to help finance the farm from year one *and* grow his own capital. He had liquidity, control, and peace of mind.

He wasn't waiting for some magic moment in the future. He was building financial freedom in real time.

This example shows how a dividend-paying whole life insurance policy (based on the current dividend scale in 2025) could work in a case similar to Jake's. In this example, the policy owner puts $50,000 in as premiums for ten years and then stops adding premiums. This example shows how the cash value and death benefit grew in the first ten years and continued after the premium payments were stopped.

Year	Annual Premiums Paid	Cash Value	Death Benefit
1	$50,000	$44,609	$1,658,000
2	$50,000	$94,178	
3	$50,000	$147,144	
4	$50,000	$202,856	
5	$50,000	$261,392	$2,437,000
6	$50,000	$325,413	
7	$50,000	$391,295	
8	$50,000	$463,194	
9	$50,000	$540,903	
10	$50,000	$621,151	$2,690,000
15	$0	$805,448	$2,834,000
20	$0	$1,043,405	$3,047,000
25	$0	$1,342,132	$3,332,000
30	$0	$1,740,137	$3,697,000
35	$0	$2,265,970	$4,159,000

The Long View

At first glance, Ray looked like he was winning. His savings grew faster in the early years, but that was only because the bank was already built. Jake's system needed time, just like planting alfalfa on a new section of land. Slow to start, but once the roots took hold, the growth came quickly and quietly, year after year.

Each passing year, life happened, just like it does to your family. Jake had access via policy loans as the farm tried to grow and tackle the same weather and price fluctuations that Ray had to deal with. Ray had access to cash. Every dollar he withdrew helped solve a problem in that year but sacrificed the compound effect of his future.

By year fifteen, Jake's cash value had outpaced Ray's. By year twenty, he had over $1 million and a $3 million death benefit. By year thirty-five, the numbers told a story Ray could no longer ignore: $2.2 million in liquid cash value and a death benefit of over $4 million. Meanwhile, Ray had watched his savings rise and fall with the markets, the weather, and the whims of bankers.

Ray had no idea what the cost of insuring his life to age eighty-five would be using term insurance—until it was too late. Most people cancel their term policies before the life insurance company ever pays a dime. They don't outlive their premiums. They *outlive the policy*.

Jake? His coverage would never expire. If a truck took him off the road at seventy-two, the next generation wouldn't just get land. They'd get capital, tax-free. His farm wouldn't just survive; it would expand.

The Real Crop You're Growing

This story isn't about money. It's about control. It's about whether you want to *own* the barn or just *rent* the tools. Whether you want to build something that lasts beyond your lifetime or stay at the mercy of interest rates, loan officers, and the next crisis you didn't see coming.

Ray and Jake still wave at each other on the gravel road and still see each other at the co-op, but their futures couldn't be more different.

Ray's got a good farm. Jake's got a good farm, but he's building a legacy.

The only difference? One man saw banking as something you had to go through. The other saw it as a process you could *own*.

So ask yourself: Which farmer do you want to be?

Jake's Ledger Notes

Day 1 – "Planted the seed. Paid my first premium. Didn't feel like much at first, but neither did that first rain."

Day 30 – "Used my first policy loan to buy seed, pay some wages, and fix the header. All my cash value is still growing inside the policy like nothing happened."

Years 1 through 10 – "Accessed policy loans for the things we needed and repaid them without draining any of my cash value reserves. Bankers stopped calling. I stopped answering."

Year 15 – "Cash value hit $800,000. I only ever paid $500,000 in premiums. My system's working harder than ever—and I'm sleeping better at night."

"My grandkids won't just inherit land. They'll inherit options."

5

The Family Grain Bin

Picture the grain bin on your farm (or a neighbor's if you don't have one).

Its metal sheets gleam under the sun as it stands tall and sturdy, a silent guardian over your farm. Each dent or scratch tells a story of years spent standing firm over your crops, livestock, and family, but the most important part of this grain bin lies inside.

Harvested grain or animal feed is stored safely within, protected from the weather and rodents. It keeps the grain dry and at the right temperature, preserving its quality until you choose to sell or use it. It allows you to stock up when prices are low or wait to sell until prices are favorable, giving you the freedom to act on your own timeline. This powerful decision-making potential is often overlooked as a key element to your ability to maximize profit.

What would you do without it?

Lacking that security, you'd be at the mercy of external factors.

Just as the grain bin shields your resources, IBC acts as a safeguard that protects your money. With your own banking system, your money is safely stored in your policies, ready to be taken out whenever you're ready to borrow it.

The grain bin allows you to warehouse something precious while also protecting it from well-known and consistent risks that you have little to no control over (like rodents and weather).

Just like the grain in your bin, you do not have to be physically holding your cash to say it's yours. You retain ownership over it no matter where it is. Using the product of participating dividend-paying your whole life is about protecting you.

The ongoing volatility of stock and real estate markets, fertilizer prices, interest rate fluctuations, and even inflation are putting pressure on every dollar you have to earn. Using this structure of whole life provides the "metal sheets" of protection around your capital in regard to these diverse and challenging forces you have no direct control over.

Think about it: does the following paragraph describe a grain bin or an Infinite Banking system?

The more you put in, the more you can take out later. Everything you store inside is readily available whenever you want to access it, and it is sheltered from outside dangers. It supports your whole family and gives you a safety net you can rely on.

That paragraph could easily describe both!

Consider how unpredictable market prices are. One day, they may be low, and the next, they're through the roof. Without a grain bin, you may be forced to sell when you can't get as much profit or to buy when it's out of your price range.

With a grain bin, you can save your grain to sell until you can get the best profit, or buy when you get the best deal.

In the same way, when you use IBC, you are capitalizing on the opportunity cost. Opportunity cost is simply described as the loss you experience by choosing a different option. In this case, if you sold your grain immediately because you didn't have a grain bin, you would lose the money you could have earned by waiting.

In the case of IBC, you store your funds in this system until you need them. Since you're paying interest back to the life insurance company you co-own while your cash value continues to grow uninterrupted, you gain access to more money. Now, contrast this with borrowing from a third party. IBC is your own Family Grain Bin[IP].

Consider opportunity cost another way. What happens if you take a week off and shut down the farm in the middle of the harvest season? You harvest fewer crops, which means less revenue. Imagine doing that every harvest. It adds up.

Now, apply that to your finances. Every time you use an outside lender, you lose the interest volume forever. Borrowing from a bank instead of your own system is like planting crops but never harvesting them!

Think about how much has passed through your hands up until now. You earn and spend a lot of money, but you most likely don't keep it. Just like increasing the amount of land you farm raises your potential revenue, retaining more of your cash flow—both principal and interest—for a longer period can drastically increase your profit potential.

Expanding Your Financial Family Grain Bin

When managing a farm, the key to success is found in collaboration. You are not just planting crops or raising livestock on your own; your team works together from planting to harvest and all the unexpected challenges in between.

Interpersonal skills are some of the most important skills a farmer can learn. Especially on small- to medium-sized farms, you must lead family or farmhands in completing daily tasks, ready to ask questions or resolve issues. Effective communication, coaching, and compassion are vital for motivating helpers to produce efficiently.

Interpersonal skills also aid you during interactions with associates and buyers. As a good farmer, you are able to negotiate the best rates for your crop yields and animals. You build a support network within the community that allows access to supplies, hay bales, and leased equipment.

That's the same power IBC provides for you and your farm. Your money pool isn't just for you but for anyone in your system. Sure, if you just have one policy, you can build up some wealth. However, it's when you have multiple policies on various loved ones that you can truly grow your capital.

Think of what might happen if you decide to expand your grain bin. Your farm has taken off, and you've purchased a neighboring plot of land, either to plant more crops or raise more livestock. With an increased harvest, you should invest in a second grain bin or expand your existing one, allowing you to hold more at one time. You pay off your grain bin with your banking system, and then you are ready for more income.

When you fill the bin and run out of room, you have to invest in setting up another one to store and protect excess grain. No farmer has ever said, "Gee, I wish I didn't have this much harvest to store; if only my fields produced less value, then I wouldn't need to buy more storage bins." That would be a preposterous idea!

With IBC, expanding your storage facilities simply means applying for a new participating policy on yourself or another family member. In fact, often when working with the right team of professionals, the design of your first policy will make it easier to add another in the future. With greater access to funds and an increased death benefit, the value of adding a second policy is hard to deny.

We get it: A death benefit isn't usually something you want to think about. Hopefully, you will have to wait many years before someone passes away. The truth is, it will happen. When it does, you will have that death benefit to provide a buffer that supports you and your farm without rushing you into debt. The more policies you have in your system, the higher the death benefit, and the more you can borrow while the insured person is still alive.

Planning for future growth is prudent and a critical conversation to have with your coach early on as you start this process. By opening policies on everyone in your household, you expand your financial Family Grain Bin to open up future opportunities for yourself and your family.

In Jayson and Richard's book *Cash Follows The Leader: Uninterrupted Daily Growth with High Cash Value Life Insurance*, we outline and explain exactly how these whole life assets accumulate in cash value and the contractual nature. At a high level, the cash value asset is the present value of the future death benefit.

By age 100 in Canada and age 121 in the United States, these participating whole life contracts must equal the total whole life death benefit. Therefore, each passing year, with a combination of your premium funding decisions and the dividend you earn, the death benefit increases in large chunks. This repeating process causes forced accumulation of the cash value at an increasing pace over time.

Keep Moving Forward

Just because you put grain in your grain bin doesn't mean you have to use it all now. You store it until the time is right to use it, whether a little at a time or all at once. As long as it is still good, you can keep it until the best moment.

In the same way, your cash value in your banking system will wait until you need it. Unlike grain, it won't "expire" for as long as it's in the policy. Even if you foresee no immediate use for it, it is available for any future emergencies or planned expenses.

A word of caution is important. Sitting on all the capital while it is safe can lead to complacency. Recognize that there is great power in how many times you can turn over a dollar, just like inventory in your local grocery store.

Owning a grain bin also doesn't mean you stop collecting or buying once you put some in. You need to make sure you add more grain into your bin, no matter how much is already there. This is especially true if you start to take some out. You're used to steady access to grain, but that only happens if you consistently stock your supply.

Can you imagine what would happen if you only took without replenishing?

Eventually, you'd run out and be stuck, especially if a drastic market shift made it more expensive or if foul weather decreased your harvest. Your livestock would starve, and you wouldn't be making any income to support your family.

Just like you have to keep adding more grain, you need to keep adding money to your Infinite Banking system. This takes the form of loan repayments and replenishing what you use. Maintain premiums that continually grow, and expand your system while also providing the equivalent of the annual maintenance you need on your storage facility.

Only doing the bare minimum (or, worse, not paying your premiums at all) will restrict your future access and could start putting the farm operation at risk. In a similar way, if you are not disciplined in putting cash flow back into the operating line of credit (policy loans), you risk going backward financially rather than progressing forward.

IBC is about staying ahead of where you would be if you were relying on banks.

If you've ever been to the airport, you've seen those moving walkways. Believe it or not, that is what it is like for people who do and don't use IBC.

Picture yourself walking next to the moving walkways at the same time as someone walks on them. You're both moving forward, but the other person is going to get to the end a lot faster because they have a boost provided by constant motion. If you just stood on the platform, you would move forward but at a similar pace to the person walking off the platform.

The combination of the platform and your effort (walking) is where you can clearly see the successful outcome of getting to your destination faster. This is how you need to approach controlling the banking function in your life.

In the same way, IBC is like those moving walkways. If you don't have your own banking system, you are walking on normal ground. You're watching other people get there faster, no matter how quickly you try to walk. All you have to do is step onto the walkways to gain control over the capital you're losing. We refer to this as the Momentum Platform[IP].

**Build your financial Family Grain Bin today,
and reap the rewards tomorrow.**

Just like your grain bin, IBC serves as a protected storage facility and a buffer to prepare you with all the resources you need to face unexpected challenges. Both require careful planning and replenishment to ensure long-term success.

By thinking of IBC as a grain bin, you gain the freedom to make decisions based on your own timeline without the pressure of outside lenders. You take advantage of opportunity cost, just as you would by waiting for the right moment to sell your crops. When you continually add to your system, you are building a strong financial foundation that supports both your present and future needs.

Imagine the power of stepping onto the moving walkway that IBC provides—no longer walking on the ground where others are passing. With every dollar you contribute to your policy, you're accelerating toward your financial goals. Keep moving forward, and remember, the more you put in, the more you'll have to access later.

6

Weeding Out Confusion with Family Banking Meetings

"There is not enough information about succession planning and farming."

Dan has heard his clients echo this concern countless times. It's an anxiety that looms large for many families. No matter how much they worry about the future, they don't know how to discuss this now.

But, guess what?

Avoiding these conversations only makes everything harder for you in the future. It may be uncomfortable or unknown, but the adverse consequences that doing so has on the future of your farm could be the difference between success and failure.

That's why the Family Banking Meeting^{IP} is a game changer.

Simply put, these meetings are about bringing together everyone in your family or business to discuss how the system has been working, what questions everyone has, and how you can grow in the future.

When everyone is on the same page, you can be safe and relaxed in the knowledge that your farm's future will be transferred to the next generation.

The Conversation That Changes Everything

We get it. Getting your entire family to sit down and talk about finances can be a challenge. There will always be people who show up late or cancel last minute, and schedules are difficult to align.

Here's the thing: Family Banking Meetings are vital for the health of a banking system.

Think about how you have to make routine repairs on your farm. When buildings, plumbing, mechanical equipment, or tools face sudden breakdowns, you have to fix them yourself or call in repair professionals.

By making routine repairs before the damage reaches this point, you are setting yourself up to avoid these headaches and hopefully save some money in the process. Not only that, but it saves you the time you'd otherwise have spent waiting to be able to use your tools again.

In the same way, you don't want to wait to address problems until your family suddenly has urgent questions. You make repairs as you go, address questions or concerns as they pop up, and keep teaching the basic policies. Have these conversations before they are necessary.

Another big reason to hold family meetings is to ensure your system outlives you.

Imagine you spend your whole life working on your farm, but when you pass, the farm goes to some stranger outside of your family. All your hard work benefits someone else.

It's the same situation with your banking system. Without discussing how to keep the system functioning, your family will lose it after you're gone. All the money and potential to save future generations will disappear.

It's like something Nelson Nash once said about corn, "When you plant corn, you're going to get weeds. Imagine you have so many weeds that you can't see the corn."

If you got rid of those weeds, wouldn't the corn stand out?

You will hear a lot of things about IBC and finances, and you and others in your system may feel overwhelmed. By opening the floor for questions and comments, you are letting people sort through the weeds (misinformation and misunderstandings) that have started growing in their minds.

How to Run a Meeting

We are often asked who should be invited to a banking meeting.

Everyone involved in your business should be there. Some may have policies in place, but you should also invite anyone who may be interested (such as other family members who are curious but undecided) and anyone who might be affected by the decisions.

One of Dan's clients is working with her husband to develop a farm located between their two family farms—his parents own one on one side, and her parents own one on the other. While she and her husband contribute significantly to her family's farm, her brother is not involved. As a result, she is concerned about whether her parents will treat them fairly in the eventual division of the farm.

In this situation, this client and her husband should be at the meeting, but so should her parents. Even though they aren't part of the banking system, they are directly involved in the health and longevity of the farm, and they want these conversations to happen now so everyone is prepared in the future.

In short, all stakeholders in the farm should be there so that the right conversations can begin immediately.

Once you pick a date and location, you can plan an agenda. Decide what you will discuss ahead of time, but try to leave plenty of space for questions and comments.

Before starting the meeting, make sure to rid your space of distractions and have everyone turn off their phones. This should be a time when everyone is focused, and the risk of a phone call or a text message could derail the meeting for everyone involved. You can keep a phone if you want a record of the meeting for anyone who can't make it.

Start your meetings by going over the goals for your banking system and tying this into the big picture of keeping the farm with the family.

What do you want to achieve with your bank? What needs to be done to get there? You want to be thinking about how you can use this system in the future.

Then, you can share any triumphs. By recognizing those who have paid off a loan or made a significant purchase, you are encouraging them to keep up their good work and to follow the family banking system rules, like paying back loans on time. Both demonstrating and celebrating this activity is leading by example.

You are setting the precedent of how you expect everyone involved to treat the system. Use analogies that connect to your specific farming operation, especially ones that connect to responsibility, accountability, and prudent management.

As we said, you should also open the floor for questions. As simple as the concept is, people might be confused about little things, especially if they overthink them. Encourage questions, explain the answers, and follow up later to make sure everyone who asked a question understands the response.

Don't worry, you do not need to be an expert on everything; this book can serve as a tool in your toolbox in addition to the bonus resources you can access using the link below. Let our team help you as you leverage what we have already built to educate your loved ones slowly but surely.

growyourowncapital.com/bonus

One of the most important things you can do during the meeting is to read part of *Becoming Your Own Banker*. Find one section (a couple of pages maximum) to read together and then discuss. This book is quite simply the best IBC resource out there because it comes right from Nelson Nash himself. Never stop going back to the source.

Before you finish your meeting, talk about any upcoming uses for the system. For example, let your brother share how he wants to finance a new truck, or encourage your nephew to announce that he will pay off his loan by the end of next month.

At the end, set the stage for everyone to share a take-away, win, or positive moment. This will help them associate something happy with IBC and will encourage them as they prepare to continue the system on their own.

We also like to follow the meeting with something fun, like a family game, cake, or a big meal. Sometimes, we even go on a family vacation for our meeting. This is especially helpful for kids, who might get bored during the meetings.

People recall positive memories and love to share about fun and engaging experiences they have had. By intentionally creating this culture, you are setting up a win before you have even started. Conversations about money can be fun if you create the right environment.

Effective discussions aren't just what you talk about; they're also how and when you come together. Finding the right time makes all the difference.

Meetings should be held at least once a year. You can do it more frequently (i.e., every quarter or every six months), but be careful not to overdo it, or you won't be able to see a difference by your next meeting.

You should aim for an hour-long meeting, or thirty minutes if it involves young children, to start. As more members get involved and your system grows, you will naturally recognize if you need to expand these meetings as well.

And yes, kids should absolutely be involved in this. They often learn the system much faster, and getting them involved early will help them stick with it later. We have some exercises you can consider doing with kids of various ages if you pick up a copy of our fourth book, *Don't Spread the Wealth*.

The biggest takeaway about Family Banking Meetings is that you are always learning. Even we learn new ways to use this process when we hear what our clients are doing. That's why it's called "infinite"; we never want to stop learning.

These meetings give you the chance to learn, share, and grow as you dive into these topics together and celebrate each other's triumphs. You can learn from the confusion and questions of others at the same time as you hear other people's answers and wisdom.

The discussions you have at your meetings will cultivate a whole new way of thinking, and future generations of your family will thank you for it.

PART THREE

Harvest

7

Stories from the Field

You can tell a farmer the yield is better across the fence, but until they walk through that field, until they see the crop with their own eyes, it's all just talk. So, let's walk the field.

These are real farmers. People with dirt under their nails and diesel in their veins. People who were tired of watching their hard-earned dollars leave the farm and never return. What they did next changed everything, not just for them, but for the generations coming behind them.

Marty and Wendy

Marty and Wendy didn't grow up in the same world. He was raised on generations of grit and tractors. She built her farming knowledge from scratch—lesson by lesson, season by season—while teaching school to keep the bills paid.

However, they shared one thing: a dream that the farm would not just survive but thrive.

1,760 acres, two kids under ten, and enough debt to make most people break into a sweat. Each spring, they'd borrow $500,000 just to keep the wheels turning so they could buy seed, fuel, repairs, equipment, and groceries. A farm like that doesn't run on hope but on capital.

That $500,000 was borrowed from someone else's bank in someone else's control. Every time a payment left their account, it was money permanently transferred away from the farm. Gone. Not growing.

But Marty and Wendy are dreamers with a clear vision for the future.

They want to expand their farm. They aspire to own and control their annual operating loan within ten years, freeing themselves from dependence on the bank.

Wendy wanted off the treadmill, more time with the kids, more hands in the soil, not grading papers. They wanted to retire with dignity and leave the next generation a path that didn't begin with debt.

So they did the uncommon. They took $50,000 a year, half of it from Wendy's school salary, and put it into dividend-paying whole life policies. No longer into someone else's bank but into their own.

They began taking unstructured policy loans. No repayment calendar. No banker peering over the fence. They paid back when they sold grain, and not a day earlier.

By the end of the ten years, Marty and Wendy expect to control their $500,000 operating loan through their private banking system. They will have access to over $1,076,915 in cash value after twenty years, having contributed $621,000 in premiums.

By year thirty, their cash value will exceed $1.8 million, with total premiums paid amounting to $743,000.

Their plan extends beyond securing their operating loan. By using this system, they'll also have the flexibility to expand their farm. Wendy will be able to stop teaching and dedicate more time to farming, as they both envision.

The life insurance policies will also provide a death benefit—a tax-free wealth transfer that will ensure their family's financial security.

In their retirement years, Marty and Wendy will be able to tap into their funds for passive income, supporting themselves without placing pressure on the farm. They will also have the resources to help their children should they choose to farm, passing down not only their land but also their knowledge of this strategy.

Marty and Wendy are not only building wealth for themselves but are also creating a legacy for their children. They are teaching them about the process of financial independence, ensuring that the next generation will inherit both their farmland and a deep understanding of how to control their financial destiny.

Through careful planning, commitment, and the implementation of a sound strategy, Marty and Wendy are well on their way to achieving their dreams of a secure, self-sustaining future.

Rachel and Josh

Rachel and Josh didn't just fall into farming. They fought for it. Rachel was the first in her family to farm, and Josh carried the weight of three generations before him. Together, they were committed to not being the last.

They manage 1,920 acres in the Midwest (640 rented and 1,280 owned) and raise three kids under eleven while juggling unpredictable seasons and the ever-growing costs of farming.

Each year, their input loan—a critical operating expense—requires $300,000, a sum that stretches their budget and puts significant pressure on their long-term plans. Rising costs, unpredictable weather, and the ever-present risks of agriculture only add to the stress. Every dollar comes with strings attached: due dates, collateral requirements, and the constant threat of "we'll need to re-evaluate this loan next year."

They love the life they've built and are determined to protect their family legacy.

They don't just want to survive the season. They want to pass on the family name with the land still attached. They know that means changing how money moves on their farm.

Seeking a way to break free from reliance on traditional banking and to mitigate the strain of their growing debts, Rachel and Josh began exploring their options. They stumbled upon the concept of Infinite Banking, pulled in by the idea of taking control of their input loan and financial future.

After doing their homework, they decided to take the plunge. Their goal was clear: Over ten years, they would use the Infinite Banking strategy to eliminate their dependence on commercial banks for their operating loans. Additionally, they planned to free up the collateral tied to their loans, giving them more flexibility to pursue other opportunities.

With a clear vision in mind, they each began to fund dividend-paying whole life insurance policies, contributing $15,000 per year.

Almost immediately, they tapped into the potential of these policies, borrowing against them to reduce the size of their input loan. In the first year alone, they were able to reduce their loan from the commercial bank by $20,000.

As the farming season progressed and the crops were harvested in the fall, Rachel and Josh used the flexibility of their policies to decide when it was best to pay off their policy loans, setting themselves up for success in the following year.

This newfound freedom gave them more control over their cash flow, allowing them to make better decisions regarding when to sell their crops in order to maximize profits.

Six years into their journey, Rachel and Josh's decision to pay their life insurance premiums each spring has paid off. They've built up enough capital within their policies to cover half of their annual input loan, and based on their current trajectory, they anticipate being able to cover the entire $300,000 loan by year ten.

As they continue to plan for the future, Rachel and Josh have decided to pay their premiums for at least fourteen years, with the ability to grow it even more if they keep going. By then, they will have accumulated over $475,000 in their policies—an amount that will continue to grow each year.

After the fourteenth year, Rachel and Josh plan to stop paying premiums out of pocket unless they have a windfall event. Instead, they will use the dividends from their policies to sustain them for the rest of their lives. They know that they have the option to continue contributing if they wish, but for now, they are comfortable with their decision.

In recent conversations, both Rachel and Josh have expressed satisfaction with the progress made. They are excited for the day when they will no longer need the commercial bank for operating loans and are confident that they've set themselves up for financial freedom.

As devoted farmers, Rachel and Josh are deeply invested in the future of their farm. They dream of the day when one or more of their children will step into their shoes, carrying on the family tradition of farming. When that time comes, they plan to use the cash value of their policies to provide income for themselves, reducing the financial burden on the farm.

Final Rows

What both couples have done is simple. They've taken control. They've stopped exporting their wealth and started harvesting it. No longer are they letting traditional banks or outside institutions dictate the terms of their financial future. Instead, they're making sure they have a legacy to leave their children, one that can last for generations.

Their farm will prosper long after they're gone, not because of luck or good land but because of the choices they're making today for the benefit of their family.

IBC didn't give them riches overnight. It gave them something better: certainty in uncertainty, control within a chaotic world, and quiet confidence that silences fear. It gave them the ability to say, "We'll figure it out," and actually mean it. It's a system that grows deeper roots with each passing season.

8

Farming for the Future

We've said it before: IBC is not about becoming rich overnight. It's a process that builds up your wealth over time.

It's a way that gives you lasting prosperity.

Think about how we're accustomed to instant gratification. With technology, we have access to whatever we want at a moment's notice. From ordering delivery right to our door to looking up our weirdest questions to chatting with people across the world, we are used to having things right now.

We used to have to wait until after the film was full to even look at our pictures. Now, we can hardly wait a few seconds!

In the same way, we desire to build wealth *now*, but that mindset often puts our money in risky situations that may not be helpful in the long run. When it comes to behavior that will make a difference financially, we need to make changes today to benefit the future. By setting aside portions of your income, it can grow for future use, much like how planting seeds now will grow into harvestable crops later.

Think of someone in your life who had a positive impact on you.

For Dan, it was his grandfather. When he grew up on the family farm, Gramps was always there. Don't you think it matters to Dan when he talks about his grandchildren?

Because IBC is about looking to the future. Dan is building up capital that future generations can use. As Proverbs 13:22 says, "A good person leaves an inheritance for their children's children."

Who in your life would you like to leave a future inheritance to? You may not have children or grandchildren, but there are likely people (like farmhands or business partners) to whom you could pass your wealth.

Dan's Fishy Story

Clients often ask me: Why start now?

To that, I ask, why *not* start now? You make payments often, maybe even daily. Every single time you make a purchase, you are missing out on that opportunity cost, as we talked about in Chapter 5.

When in Playa del Carmen for my daughter's wedding in 2010, we took a guy's fishing trip. We were on the water waiting for a fish until finally, one bit the line. I was chosen to be the one who took it (probably because I was paying the bill!). The captain told us if we wanted to reel it in, we had to keep it and have it preserved by a taxidermist.

Do you know how much it ended up costing me at the time?

It was about $3,500 by the time I got it home!

But, how much did it really cost me?

If you consider a 30 percent tax rate, I had to earn $5,000 to pay $3,500. That was nearly fifteen years ago, and with the lost opportunity cost, you can add nearly $2,000 more. I lost the opportunity to use that cash for anything for the rest of my life.

If I had already been implementing the Infinite Banking Concept, used a policy loan to pay for that purchase, and then paid it back over time, I would have been able to use all the money again, putting it to work for me in other ways.

This is the reality you face: You're going to deal with major expenses. What kind of system you have can mean the difference between a short-term cost and a long-term liability.

However, it doesn't stop there. Now that I have my system, I need to put that money to work.

How do my wife and I generate passive income? We lend the insurance companies money we access from our system. Some of this private lending is to family and some to third parties (we can take collateral just like a regular bank can).

My youngest daughter has used the system for cars, car maintenance, and trips. Instead of putting that on a credit card, she calls up the family banker, who just so happens to be me. We discuss, plan, and work out a proper payment arrangement.

My son has used it for trucks. He was even able to take a break from his payments while he changed jobs, a flexibility that third-party loans don't allow. As the banker in this scenario, I get to make the rules, but he still has to make up the payments and any accrued interest. Rules are important for successful long-term implementation.

My second-oldest daughter started a business and bought a home with our family banking system. This house was the biggest expense we've funded.

The benefits will continue to be helpful in the future. When I die, my family gets more than I put in, a legacy I can leave them when I'm gone. What is the key? It's not the tax-free death benefit check, it's actually the lessons, interactions, and stewardship we are building. The memories and connection of working together and keeping more of our hard-earned money where it belongs, with the family.

This is a legacy to be proud of, and one that I can feel confident in cascading to future generations that follow when I am gone.

My family is ahead of the game financially, and it's all thanks to IBC.

Pay Yourself First

Paying yourself first doesn't mean spending right now; it means paying into your banking system so you have more money in the future. Essentially, by depositing in your policy, you are paying your future self first before you spend even a single dollar today.

We get it. It's not always as easy as it sounds. Sometimes, it can feel like you are scraping by, but if you don't make changes now, that is all your life will ever be. IBC allows you to use that capital in the future (often sooner than most people realize), and you can't do that if you aren't paying up now.

Think about where you will be in five years if you don't make any changes.

Now, think about where you *want* to be in five years.

Your need for capital will only be greater as you go through life. Don't spend all your income now. Pay your future self first. What you do now makes or breaks your financial future.

Another big way we are paying ourselves is by educating our children and grandchildren about the system.

Imagine you spent a lot of time building your family system, but you never explained how it works to your kids. If you pass away unexpectedly, they will have no idea how to run the system—and guess what happens to all that capital?

Imagine a farm family that decided their children didn't have to do any chores or help out on the farm for their entire lives. How capable would those kids be of taking over the farm one day? What desire or interest would they have in preserving what you spent a lifetime building?

In the same way, your kids won't be equipped to step in and continue to run a financial system they know nothing about. The results could be devastating as the money disappears. They likely would not take advantage of policy loans or be successful in recapturing interest.

By first involving them and then teaching them how the system works, you are ensuring a reliable financial future for your children, grandchildren, and beyond.

We always ask: what year is your policy most efficient?

It's the last one; you just don't know when that's going to be. Every year until then matters, and the sooner you start, the better that last year will be.

We can't stress this enough. This isn't just about wealth for yourself; it's for future generations.

Secure Your Farm's Future

Remember that IBC is not about whole life insurance. It's about the process. We only use whole life insurance because it is the best tool for this process.

Here's something to consider! By paying premiums into a well-structured, dividend-paying whole life insurance policy and following the principles Nelson Nash outlined in

Becoming Your Own Banker, your cash value will grow significantly beyond the premiums you've paid. This gives you access to capital for any of your needs.

Now, imagine what would happen if every person in the system did that. This wealth will be available for decades, maybe even longer.

It's a no-brainer.

You want to effectively transfer the farm to your children or grandchildren, but you may not have known how until now.

Your farm is a source of pride, and it shouldn't fall into the hands of someone on the outside, just like your money. You take risks and are hard-working; it isn't fair if your capital is lost.

With this system, you can only gain.

It's time for you to take control.

No more being unprepared for financial emergencies.

No more worrying about market fluctuations.

No more questioning if you can pass down your farm to your family.

This system is entirely in your hands. Money flows in and out, and you share your wealth with your loved ones.

Here's what I (Dan) would do differently if I could go back to 2013:

- Figure out how to put more policies on my children
- Focus more on putting my cash values to work
- Have more Family Banking Meetings to share the message

It's a simple process, and when done right, it is life-changing. Open more policies, pay as much as you can, and share that knowledge with everyone around you. You have heard about this amazing process, and it shouldn't stop with you. Your friends, your family, your neighbors, anyone can benefit from this.

Ultimately, creating a family banking system requires understanding and discipline. IBC is not a get-rich-quick process; with time and a little attention, you can achieve a successful harvest year after year.

We are talking about a powerful change in your life and the lives of future generations.

Once you start growing your own capital, your opportunities are endless.

What are your next steps?

It's very simple.

First, book your one-on-one meeting with a member of our world-class team of Authorized Infinite Banking Concept Practitioners, and collect your amazing bonuses!

Go to growyourowncapital.com/bonus

These resources will help you see how to implement this in your life and expand your horizons even further. Working directly with a qualified coach on our team will show you the way to get started, help you set up a customized plan for your farming operation, and assist you in planning for expansion along the way.

You will get immediate access to:

- Over seven hours of video training to learn how to implement this in your life, with real-world stories included
- Dan's story of the three-generations impact he is making with his own children and grandchildren

- The FarmBanker Legacy Planner[IP] workbook to start putting what you have learned into action and build the plan that is right for your farming family
- Tools to teach you why you are never too old to start and how you can do this in your sixties and beyond
- An estate planning session for farm families with Dan Allen and Certified Financial Planner Chris Thomson
- And so much more!

This training will become your farm's financial defence system!

Secondly, subscribe to our podcast, Wealth On Main Street, using your favourite podcast player: wealthonmain-street.com

Just as you watch the weather reports and keep tabs on commodity prices, you will continue to learn and grow from this process by tuning into new episodes of our podcast. Every week, you can listen in from the tractor to expand your financial knowledge, generate life-changing ideas, and hear real stories of everyday people just like you implementing this powerful strategy.

We are here to support you on this incredible journey, and we are excited about what the future holds for you and your family's legacy.

About the Authors

Dan Allen grew up on a mixed farm where he was involved in everything from milking cows and raising cattle and hogs to all the activities with growing cash crops. After high school, Dan studied agriculture before returning to the family farm where he worked for the next fourteen years.

Dan was introduced to IBC in 2013 and started to personally practice it in 2014. Dan started to train as an IBC practitioner in 2016 and has been coaching others in the concept ever since.

Jayson Lowe is the founder of The Lowe Group of Companies, including the Wealth On Main Street Podcast and Ascendant Financial Inc. A visionary and a gifted leader, he has over twenty-two years of experience as a highly regarded coach, speaker, and advisor to individuals and business owners nationwide.

When he's not building the Ascendant Financial organization he owns with his wife,

Rebecca, Jayson enjoys spending quality time with his four children.

Richard Canfield is an Authorized Infinite Banking Practitioner and co-host of the Wealth On Main Street Podcast. He is passionate about helping families take more control over their financial lives.

When not helping others, Richard enjoys spending time with his two kids and his amazing wife, Heather. He loves the mountains, time at the lake/beach, anything with a zipline, and busting out tools for random household projects. He strives to learn new things and always seeks personal growth.

Ready for a Conversation? Schedule Today

WealthOnMainStreet.com/BookACall

CONNECT WITH RICHARD, JAYSON & DAN TODAY

WEALTH ON
MAIN STREET

WealthOnMainStreet.com/Authors

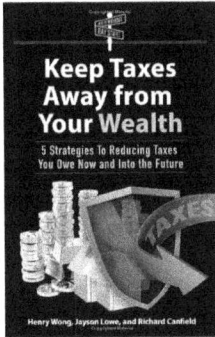

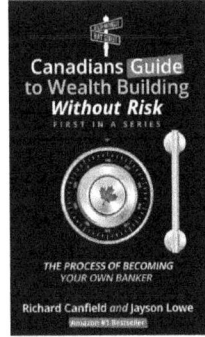

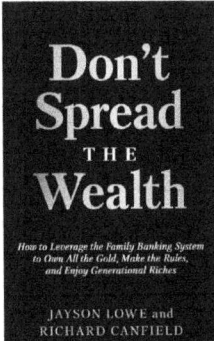

www.ingramcontent.com/pod-product-compliance
Lightning Source LLC
Chambersburg PA
CBHW071439210326
41597CB00020B/3861